Rapid Reading Series

# A Bright Knight
## Book 13

Written by G. Grafi
©2021

For Ben Ben:
You have always been a son
to me. I am so proud of the
man you have become!

A note to parents and teachers:
This is the thirteenth  book in
the Rapid Reading series. Its
purpose is to practice the "ight"
word family.

Follow the guide and use the
tables on the next page to
practice the "ight" words prior
to reading the book in order to
facilitate the reading process.

Sight words are high frequency
words that often repeat
themselves in many beginning
books. Sight words are
remembered rather than read.
It is recommended to practice
sight words as well.

*Dr. G. Grafi*

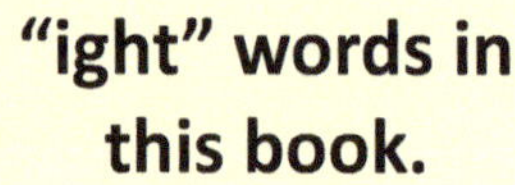

## "ight" words in this book.

| | | |
|---|---|---|
| Bright | delightful | mighty |
| sunlight | sights | knight |
| flight | midnight | Dwight |
| plight | light | height |
| tonight | fright | twilight |
| right | might | fight |
| tight | flashlight | night |

## Sight Words in this book.

| | |
|---|---|
| lady | knight |
| loves | there |
| doesn't | was |
| one | dragon |
| has | won |
| away | until |
| saw | become |
| horse | |

This is Lady Br*ight*.
She loves the sunl*ight*.

She doesn't like flights, and
no one sees her plight.

Ton**ight**, she has a fl**ight**
to a far away land.
It feels r**ight**!

On the flight, she will
hold on tight.

In the far away land, she saw many delightful sights.

One night Lady Bright went to a ball till midnight.

There was no light and
Lady Bright had a fright.

She held on to her horse
tight with all her might.

She looked with the light
from her flashlight.

Lady Bright saw there was a mighty knight.

The knight's name
was Dwight.

Lady Bright saw the knight's height in the twilight.

It was a sight to see the fight with the dragon.

Lady Bright and the knight took flight right when the dragon won the fight.

Lady Bright had a fight with the dragon when she saw the knight's plight.

The knight was delighted to see Lady Bright fight until after the night.

Lady Bright felt delight
when she saw that she
won the fight.

Lady Bright chose to become a knight.

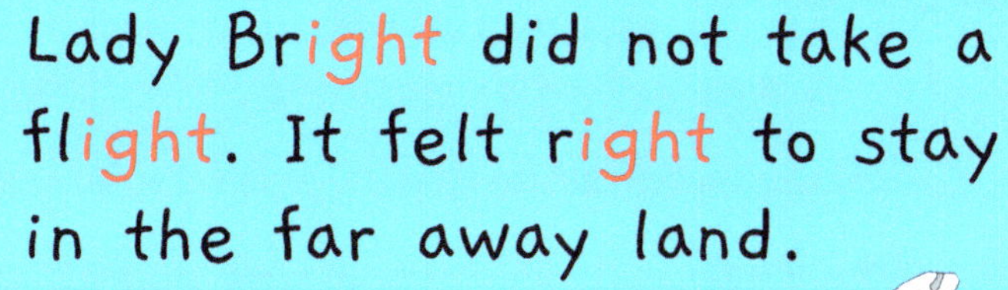

Lady Bright did not take a flight. It felt right to stay in the far away land.

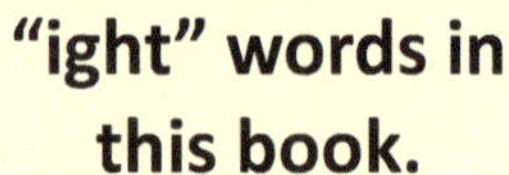



| | | |
|---|---|---|
| Bright | delightful | mighty |
| sunlight | sights | knight |
| flight | midnight | Dwight |
| plight | light | height |
| tonight | fright | twilight |
| right | might | fight |
| tight | flashlight | night |

## Sight Words in this book.

| | |
|---|---|
| lady | knight |
| loves | there |
| doesn't | was |
| one | dragon |
| has | won |
| away | until |
| saw | become |
| horse | |